Contents

Introduction   4
Dance in education   5
The lesson   6

ACTION TIME
Action time diagram   9
Statues   10
Ready, steady, go!   11
Listen, listen to the feet   12

THE ELEMENTS
The elements diagram   14
Earth   15
Wind   17
Fire   19
Water   21

PATTERNS AND PATHWAYS
Patterns and pathways diagram   23
Air and floor patterns   24
Follow-my-leader pathways   25
Circles and spirals   26
An imaginary journey   27

MAGIC AND MYSTERY
Magic and mystery diagram   28
The haunted house   29

Ghostly creatures   30
Magic moments   31
Night-time shadows   32

ANIMALS
Animals diagram   33
Cats   34
The zoo   35
Carnival of the animals   36

MINIBEASTS
Minibeasts diagram   38
Minibeasts   39
The birth of a butterfly   40
Pond life   41
The spider and the fly   42

CARNIVAL TIME
Carnival time diagram   43
Clowns   44
A fancy-dress parade   45
A carnival fairground   46
The carnival parade   47

APPENDIX
Dance evaluation sheet   48

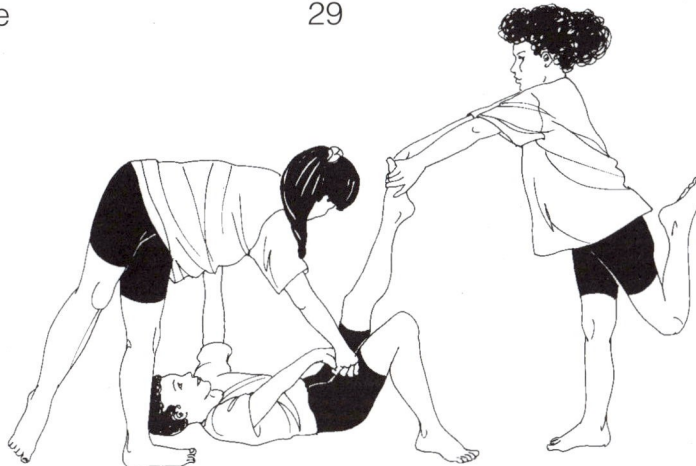

Introduction

This book aims to provide a simple, structured way of gaining access to the potential for expressive movement and dance. The focus is on the 7–11 age range, but most of the ideas can be adapted to many ages and abilities.

The book contains some of the theory and much of the practice involved in dance teaching. Each 'action idea' has possibilities for further development (see progression on each page). The ideas and activities are grouped into sections. At the beginning of each section there is a chart showing the contents, which will enable cross-curricular links to be made.

The book invites teachers to observe what the children do and to appreciate and to build upon their efforts. As their confidence and experience increase, they will spontaneously put forward their own ideas and develop these ideas in their own way.

Each 'action idea' suggests ways to improve the quality of movement by using images such as 'creep quietly and slowly like a cat' or 'pounce suddenly like a lion'. Improve quality and co-ordination of movement by asking questions such as 'Can you reach a little bit higher?' or

'Stretch your fingers and toes more'. In other words, assume responsibility for the quality control.

The book aims to build confidence and trust between the children, the teacher and the dance ideas. Eventually the words should become unnecessary because the ideas are merely starting points that the children explore and experiment with to find new ways of expressing themselves physically.

There is no single way to introduce dance to children. The ideas on the activity sheets are intended to stimulate rather than dictate. Most teachers as well as children need practical advice and some degree of success before they have the confidence and competence to allow themselves and others total freedom in any art form.

All the dance ideas have been tried and tested successfully by a wide range of teachers and children. They have provided easy access to dance teaching with boys and girls aged 7–11. The photocopied activity sheets will help any teacher to deliver an exciting creative session with the minimum of effort.

FOLENS PE

Dance

Kate Harrison

Acknowledgements

Folens allows photocopying of pages marked 'copiable page' for educational use, providing that this use is within the confines of the purchasing institution. Copiable pages should not be declared in any return in respect of any photocopying licence.

Folens books are protected by international copyright laws. All rights are reserved. The copyright of all materials in this book, except where otherwise stated, remains the property of the publisher and author. No part of this publication may be reproduced, stored in a retrieval system, or transmitted, in any form or by any means, for whatever purpose, without the written permission of Folens Limited.

This resource may be used in a variety of ways. However, it is not intended that teachers or children should write directly into the book itself.

Kate Harrison hereby asserts her moral rights to be identified as the author of this work in accordance with the Copyright, Designs and Patents Act 1988.

Editors: Alyson Jones and Andrew Brown
Illustrations: Catherine Ward – Simon Girling and Associates

Layout artist: Patricia Hollingsworth
Cover image: Leonard Defoe

© 1996 Folens Limited, on behalf of the author.

Every effort has been made to contact copyright holders of material used in this book. If any have been overlooked, we will be pleased to make any necessary arrangements.

British Library Cataloguing in Publication Data. A catalogue record for this book is available from the British Library.

First published 1996 by Folens Limited, Dunstable and Dublin.
Folens Limited, Albert House, Apex Business Centre, Boscombe Road, Dunstable, LU5 4RL, England.

ISBN 1 85276 277-2

Printed in Singapore by Craft Print.

Dance in education

Dance in education develops the children's ability to communicate through a non-verbal language – a body language.

Dance has its own vocabulary. This vocabulary can be divided into four areas:

1

Action	What can I do?
● Travelling:	run, roll, slither, creep, trot, gallop, skip, tiptoe.
● Jumping:	hop, leap, bounce.
● Turning:	spin, spiral, twirl, twist.
● Gesturing:	stretch, reach, jab, flick, wave, kick, nod, clap, pull, push, grab, hug, slap.
● Transferring weight:	step, stamp, sit, kneel, rock, sway, flop, lean collapse, fall, balance, handstand, cartwheel.

2

Space	Where can I do it?
● Direction:	forwards, backwards, sideways, straight, curved, zig-zag, up, down, across, over, under, through, near, far, towards, away from, surround.
● Size:	big, small.
● Shape:	curved, twisted, pointed, flat.

3

Dynamics	How do I do it?
● Speed:	quickly, slowly.
● Strength:	strongly, lightly.
● Rhythm:	beat, pulse.

4

Relationship   With whom do I do it?

● Alone, in pairs, small and large groups, separately and together.

● Mirroring and shadowing.

● Leader and following.

● Approach, meet, part.

● Question and answer.

Children can be trained to increase their skills in all these areas, but dancing is more than a combination of skilful actions.

The dance-making process involves the selection of the appropriate movement vocabulary.

The teacher's role

Teachers are the link between dance ideas and the children. They can see how well the children understand and perform each activity and to what extent it needs to be practised further. They can praise, encourage and comment on the quality of the children's actions. All children are very sensitive to the attitude and involvement of their teacher. Be an active participant, not a passive observer.

This does not necessarily mean taking part in the actions, but making sure that the children give their very best. The quest for quality is more easily seen than defined in words. It is achieving something never done before or doing it better than before.

Both pupil and teacher alike learn by *doing*. Together they are involved in the process of 'doing, making and looking', no matter how simple or complex the movement material may be.

The lesson structure

- Starting activities and introduction to the dance idea (warm up games and technical skills).
- Creating the dance (using movement content from the dance).
- Performing and appreciating the dance.

Warm-up activities

When choosing introductory activities try to make sure that they are, in some way, related to the chosen dance idea. Explain why an exercise or series of movements will improve the children's ability to dance, for example bending the knees when landing from jumps. Apply your knowledge of warming up safely by starting with gentle activities and progressing to more energetic, strenuous movements. Encourage the children to develop their own routine of warm-up activities using bending, stretching, twisting and swinging actions. Develop these in pairs and show each sequence to the rest of the class on a weekly basis.

Introduce the children to a range of activities that will warm up the body by:
- raising the heartbeat through walks, skips, runs, gallops and jumps
- improving flexibility and suppleness through stretching and bending the whole body as well as isolated parts of the body, for example knees and feet
- increasing stamina through sequences of jumping, skipping and travelling steps.

Dance technique is a means to an end and not an end in itself. It is the preparation for expressive dance compositions. Try to make the introductory activities seem like games, even if they involve hard technical dancework. Use games such as musical statues, follow-my-leader and 'Simon Says'. There are many more suitable suggestions for warming up in the 'Action time' and 'Patterns and pathways' sections. Some starters will also make excellent endings, so do not forget to include a 'wind down' at the end of each lesson.

Organisation before the lesson

To get the best out of the dance activities in this book prepare in the following ways:

- Provide a hall or a large space suitable for movement activities. Make sure that it is free of any obstructions and that potential sources of danger (such as pillars) are well protected. The minimum amount of space you will require for your movement sessions will allow the children to stretch their arms wide and turn around on the spot without touching anyone else.

- Ensure that the children are suitably dressed. For example, they should wear shorts or loose trousers and T-shirts. Bare feet are preferable, but if the floor is old or dirty, soft shoes should be worn. Never allow the children to wear heavy shoes, or just socks or tights as these can lead to accidents on slippery surfaces.

- Collect a few percussion instruments for your own use during the lesson (such as a drum, tambourines, bells and woodblocks). This will enable you to control the children's actions by suggesting the speed and rhythm of their movements and indicating when they should start and stop.

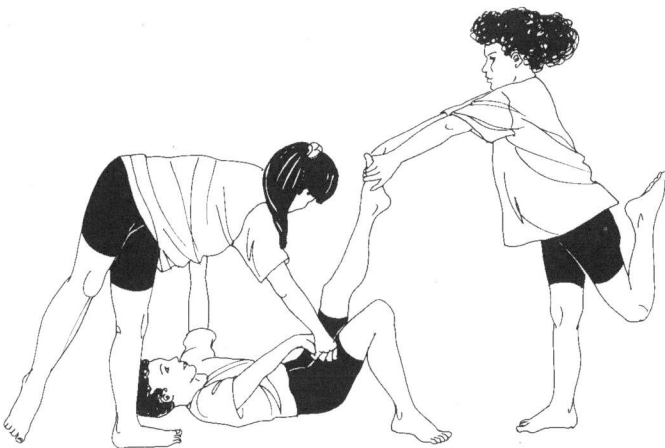

- Select a suitable musical accompaniment if necessary. Simple sounds and music can be used to stimulate and accompany movement activities (suggestions are made in the text). However, music is not essential to the succesful development of creative movement, so allow plenty of time for exploration and practice without any accompaniment. If you wish to use recorded music you will obviously need a cassette or CD player. Ensure that there is a power point and that the machine is loud enough to fill the movement area.

During the lesson

- Observe and comment on the children's responses.

- Repeat an activity if you are not satisfied with the children's work.

- Always be aware of spacing and use your initiative to prevent bunching together.

- Ensure that they start and stop on cue and that instructions are clear.

- Gather the children around you for explanations and discussion, making sure that their eyes are on you. Avoid lengthy speeches.

- Use language to clarify and enhance the action, such as: spin suddenly, step silently, creep quietly, jump, explode.

- Use open-ended questions, such as: "How does the music make you feel?"

- Ask for new ideas from the children.

- Value the responses they make to images and ideas. Encourage discussion and sharing in pairs.

- Be ready to adapt and adjust the tasks in response to the children's needs.

- Always be on the look-out for children who need help and those whom you can choose to demonstrate an activity for the others to observe. Observation helps the children to compare and contrast their efforts and to raise their standards of achievement. Look for those who have improved on their own personal standard but avoid selecting the same children each time.

- Allow time to view and appreciate the dances.

After the lesson

- Spend a few minutes considering the following:
  - was there an increase in physical skill?
  - were the set tasks differentiated and developed enough?
  - did the children respond imaginatively and inventively?
  - was dance vocabulary used (see the chart on page 5)?
  - was there sufficient depth and variety of movement or was the lesson over-prescriptive and predictable?
  - was the dance visually interesting with contrasts in level, shape and size?
  - was there a variety of action and dynamic qualities?
  - did the children perform confidently?
  - was time allowed for dance appreciation?

- Ask the children to complete the dance evaluation sheet on page 48. This could be used as a verbal or written checklist. It could include a drawing.

- Use the ideas and images as springboards to other activities. Create cross-curricular links.

- Use the ideas in the progression section as tasks that the children practise for the next lesson.

Action time

STATUES

READY, STEADY, GO!

ACTION TIME

LISTEN, LISTEN TO THE FEET 1

LISTEN, LISTEN TO THE FEET 2

This introductory section uses action rhymes as the stimulus for movement. The lessons introduce basic spacing and body activities in an enjoyable and lively way.

Statues

<table>
<tr><td>

A • I • M

To contrast stillness and movement through a series of going and stopping words.

</td><td>

RESOURCES

Travelling and stopping words
Percussion (drum)
Music (Scott Joplin's *Piano Rags* or TV/film themes)

</td></tr>
</table>

Teaching points

- Use a drum to control a simplified version of musical statues. Emphasise moving from space to space without colliding. Bang the drum to stop the action and check the spacing.
- Work on musical statues with the emphasis on stopping in a variety of body shapes at different levels.
- Vary the speed and strength of the drumbeat and encourage a variety of travelling actions, such as creeping, stamping, stepping, skipping or running.
- In pairs, one child moves in his or her own way around another child who stands still. Reverse this process.

Progression

- Develop the statues work into follow-my-leader sequences, moving alternately.
- Compose a dance with a series of four travelling and four stopping actions.
- Use music to encourage the use of imagination. Statue shapes can be the start of any creative movement activity, such as moving and stopping like clowns, animals or machines, or imitating the weather.

Forming statues in different body shapes.

Travelling words
stamp, step, march, gallop, creep, run, trot, skip

Stopping words
freeze, stop, pause, stay, hover, linger, fall

Ready, steady, go!

Teaching points

- The class should tiptoe towards and away from the centre of the room.
- Use percussion to vary the length and the speed of travel. Intersperse with statue stops.
- Find a variety of ways of slowly falling individually and then when balancing with a partner.
- Try curling quickly, then slowly. Roll and curl and then combine curling quickly with growing slowly and curling slowly with growing quickly.
- Emphasise the rhythm and use demonstrations of quality work.
- Jump on the spot in a variety of different shapes.
- Jump sideways with arms outstretched on each foot in turn. Create new rhythmic patterns.
- Experiment with balances individually, in pairs and in small groups.
- Move away from, towards or in a group shape. Move quickly, then slowly.
- Explore spiralling alone, in pairs and in small groups.

Progression

- In small groups, say the words of the poem while moving or using one child as a narrator. Find different ways of moving in a group.

RESOURCES

Action poem (below)
Percussion

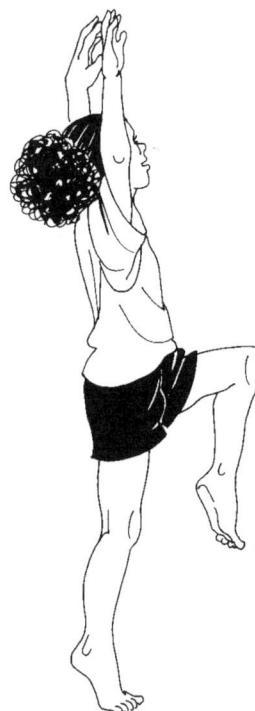

Experimenting with balances.

Ready, steady, go!

Tiptoe slowly, toe to toe,
Ready, steady slowly go,
Running quickly, not a sound,
Falling, crumpling to the ground.

Curling tightly like a ball,
Growing upwards straight and tall,
Trotting gently, knees up high,
Jumping gently, touch the sky.

Hopping now from side to side,
Balance, balance, stretched out wide,
Turning slowly, round and round,
Whirling, curling to the ground.

Listen, listen to the feet 1

To find contrasting ways
of using feet by
changing actions, speed
and strength.

Percussion (drum,
tambourine, bells)
Action poem (below)

Teaching points

- Play a strong, slow rhythmic drum beat. Contrast this with shaking bells. Ask for spontaneous interpretations on the spot, then in and out of spaces. Add surprise by unexpectedly changing from one rhythm to another.
- Contrast strong, long steps with tiny, tiptoeing steps. Create new phrases without any accompaniment.
- Explore ways of moving strongly and lightly when jumping and hopping, stamping and creeping, galloping and trotting.
- Play follow-my-leader games in pairs. The children move one at a time and 'shadow' each other. Introduce sudden stops, freezes and balances. Change leaders frequently.
- Play a question-and-answer game on the tambourine. Ask a rhythmic question that the children must answer by tapping their feet.

Progression

- In pairs, the children repeat each other's step patterns or take turns to make up rhythmic questions and answers.
- Use the rhythmic *Feet* poem. The children could react to the words individually or in pairs. Use examples to demonstrate originality and movement quality.

Taking tiny tiptoeing steps.

Feet

Listen, listen to our feet,
Big feet, small feet,
Strong feet, light feet.

Silently creeping, slowly stalking,
Toes are tapping,
Feet are talking!

Listen, listen to the feet 2

A • I • M

To develop the contrasting ways of using feet through characterisation.

RESOURCES

A tambourine
Action poem (below)

Forming a follow-my-leader line.

Teaching points

- Explore different ways of walking: forwards, backwards, sideways, with feet turned in and feet turned out, in a rhythmic phrase, both feet in unison or one after the other.
- In small groups, walk like a clown (remember a clown's footwear would change the walk). Try high knees, feet wide apart, toes turned inwards or outwards and walking on heels or with big bent knees. Suggest that a clown sometimes overbalances and work on different ways of falling and finding 'new' balancing shapes on the floor.
- Practise slow, careful stepping along straight lines with arms outstretched to balance. Put a child on each end of the 'tightrope' and take turns to balance.
- Explore a variety of leaps, turns, bounces and balances. Combine these to form acrobatic sequences.

Progression

- Form follow-my-leader lines. Step together to a slow, repeated downbeat. Change leaders and the travelling activity frequently.
- Finish with a class follow-my-leader line, dancing around the room.
- Practise the whole poem in pairs.

Feet

People walking up and down,
Funny walking like a clown,
Tightrope walkers in the sky,
Acrobats that leap and fly.

One foot, two feet, three feet, four –
Creeping creature have some more!
Feet are dancing in a line –
It's crazy caterpillar time!

The elements

EARTH 1

EARTH 2

WIND 1

WIND 2

THE ELEMENTS

FIRE 1

FIRE 2

WATER 1

WATER 2

This section uses the children's knowledge and experience of the elements as a stimulus for dynamic dances with controls in action, speed and strength.

Earth 1

A · I · M

To introduce contrasts and combinations of basic body activities – jump, run, hop, balance, fall, tiptoe.

RESOURCES

Percussion instruments
Hoops for puddles

Teaching points

- Imagine a soft springy floor and bounce, leap and jump in different directions.
- A hot, fiery floor: run and hop quickly and lightly in and out of spaces.
- A slippery floor: do stepping, balancing and falling actions, finding a variety of balances alone and with a partner.
- A wet, puddly floor: stamp, splash, leap over, tiptoe around and jump into imaginary puddles.
- A jagged, rocky floor: perform stretching, clambering, climbing and balancing actions. Try this in small groups and find several contrasting group balances.
- A sticky, muddy floor: stomp, sink or pull with strong legs and high knees. An arm, a leg or a back could get stuck and have to be pulled and pushed, to get free.

Progression

- Work in small groups to create a sequence that shows the contrasting qualities of movement that occur when the floor surface changes.

Balancing on a slippery floor.

Earth 2

<table>
<tr><td>

A ◆ I ◆ M

To explore the words 'over', 'under', 'along', 'through' and 'between' in action.

</td><td>

RESOURCES

Music
(*Tubular Bells* by Mike Oldfield)

</td></tr>
</table>

Teaching points
Around the world

- Imagine a hot, sandy desert. Pretend to draw patterns in the sand with fingers and toes curving around the body. Practise trudging through deep sand and then jumping and hopping on hot burning sand. Play follow-my-leader footprints in pairs.

- For an icy, snowy land, develop the idea of journeying using a variety of appropriate movements, such as climbing, pulling, pushing, balancing, slipping and falling. Emphasise the balances by working in pairs.

- In groups of three, imagine a gigantic jungle. Grow into tangled undergrowth shapes with stretched limbs and stand at contrasting levels with lots of space between. Encourage balance and slow changes of shape. Step carefully around, through, over and under the groups.

Progression

- Select three groups to creep carefully over, under, around and through the different tangled undergrowth shapes. Change over several times so that everyone has a chance to practise. Demonstrate originality.

Imagining a hot desert and a cold land.

Growing into tangled undergrowth.

Wind 1

To explore the
contrasting movement
qualities of the wind.

RESOURCES

Tissue paper
Action flash cards
(see list below)
Percussion or voice sounds

Teaching points
- Explore moving and stopping in and out of spaces at high and low levels.
- Vary the speed and change direction after each pause.
- Demonstrate how a piece of tissue paper reacts to the wind. Blow it to show how it might whoosh, whirl, spiral and drop.
- Explore spiralling and whirling from tall wide shapes into low, curled shapes and vice-versa. Try this on the spot and moving into spaces.

Progression
- In pairs, create a short dance on the spot and into space based on the action words on the flashcards.
- Move together, then one at a time towards, away from and around each other.

Exploring tall whirling
shapes and low
curled shapes.

Wind words
whoosh, whirl, spiral, spin, twirl, twist, drop

Wind 2

A • I • M
To further explore the contrasting movement qualities of the wind.

RESOURCES

Tissue paper
Action flash cards
(see list below)
Percussion or voice sounds

Teaching points

- Explore moving and stopping in and out of spaces at high and low levels.
- Vary the speed and change direction after each pause.
- Change the pathways from straight to curved. Add leaps and turns to increase the difficulty.
- The children could use voice sounds and hand gestures to reinforce the changing dynamics of the wind.
- Repeat the word 'drop' in as many different ways as possible, for example, quickly, slowly, strongly or lightly. The children could respond with appropriate movements.

Progression

- In groups of four, each pair could show and teach their dance to the other pair. This will make each dance twice as long.
- The children could find other ways to express the changes in the wind. They could use poems, pictures and sounds to help them.

Wind words

whoosh, whirl, spiral, spin, twirl, twist, drop

Using changing gestures to represent the wind.

Fire 1

Teaching points

Fire dances

- Ask the children to imagine that they are curling smoke. Use hands and arms to make light, curling and whirling shapes all around the body.
- For smoke rising, begin in curled body shapes and rise, turn and spread out.
- For smoke spreading, begin with large, slow curling or light, spiralling movements, rising then sinking.
- For sparks shooting, make sudden, sharp gestures using fingers, elbows and knees. Then make spiky jumps at different levels in many directions.
- For flickering flames, perform a jumping, jagged dance towards and away from each other.

Progression

- Make a sequence of these activities in groups of three.
- Create a group dance for the ending. For instance: large, slow, curling smoke or fast, fiery flames.

Pretending to be curling smoke or sudden sparks shooting.

Fire words

whirl, circle, swirl, twirl, spiral, spread, shoot, sparkle, crackle, flit, flash, dart, flicker

Fire 2

<table>
<tr><td>

A ◆ I ◆ M

To use the shape, sound and speed of fireworks to create dynamic contrasts.

</td></tr>
</table>

RESOURCES

Percussion
Voice sounds
Maracas
Handbells
Cymbal roll and crash
Drumbeat

Teaching points

Fireworks

- Imagine fireworks flashing. Sit with clenched fists, then strongly and sharply stretch and flick the fingers out in front, behind, to the sides, low and high. Repeat this standing. Add spiky jumps with bent knees on the spot and from space to space.
- Sparklers swirling: use large arm and leg gestures to create curved patterns in the air. Develop these into turning, whirling and spiralling actions.
- Rockets flying: rise slowly into tall, stretched arrow shapes, then run with 'arrowhead' fingers leading along straight pathways. Create pauses and changes in direction and finish with slow spiralling to the ground.
- Repeat this in groups of three growing into a group rocket shape, separating for the 'flight' and coming together for the final spiralling and sinking.
- 'Jumping Jacks': make small rhythmic jumps with feet together in all directions.
- 'Catherine Wheel': perform sudden spins with statue stops accompanied by voice sounds.

Progression

- Create a class firework display. In groups of three, each group will be a firework.
- Feature each different firework separately. Then finish with a class 'starburst' where fireworks 'flash' and then each trio reaches out slowly to form a huge class 'star' shape. This star stretches high and low to fingers, elbows, knees and toes.

Forming firework shapes.

Water 1

<table>
<tr><td>

A ◆ I ◆ M

To create dynamic contrasts in pairs and small groups.

</td></tr>
</table>

RESOURCES

Percussion
(tambourine, xylophone)
Water flash cards
(see list below)

Teaching points
Water music

● Water moves in all sorts of ways and makes many different patterns, shapes and sounds.

● Make sudden, light, spiky changes of shape using knees, elbows, fingers and feet. Play random notes on a xylophone.

● Use a tambourine to accompany irregular running and stopping phrases. Add 'spluttering' gestures of hands and arms.

● In pairs, create a question-and-answer sequence using light staccato jumps and strong 'splashing' jumps. The children could say the water words as they jump.

● Pairs could combine to form groups of four. Use the words to experiment with follow-my-leader lines, turning circles, pairs advancing towards and retreating away from each other, and so on.

● Work as a group turning on the spot and moving from high to low. Contrast slow spiralling with sudden spinning.

Progression
● Create a sequence using water words, percussion and the ideas above. Experiment with the groups and encourage them to create contrasts by moving on the spot and in and out of spaces.

Making water shapes.

Water words
drip, drop, splish,
splash, spray,
splatter, sprinkle, gush,
gurgle, splutter, trickle

Water 2

A ◆ I ◆ M

To create a dance in five sections based on rainfall.

RESOURCES

Voice and body sounds
A cymbal
Hoops
Music (Enya's *Watermark* or *Incantations* by Incantation)

Teaching points

Rainfall

- Experiment with phrases such as 'drip-drop', 'splish-splatter' and 'gurgle-splash' to form short sequences about rain.
- Create percussive body sounds and actions to make a rain storm.
- Try tiptoeing, jumping, running, stopping and stamping using hoops to represent puddles.
- Remind the children that the raindrops make a round, muddy, puddle. Encourage them to listen for a cymbal sound, then run towards each other to form small groups. The groups could start low and slowly grow outward to form large circular puddles. The puddle circles could shrink and grow, accompanied by the cymbal.
- In small groups, create follow-my-leader lines to form one giant puddle shape using hoops. With guidance and pausing, the lines could join on to each other.
- Finish with a free 'splashing' dance, with individuals and pairs jumping and running, tiptoeing, stamping, splashing and sploshing in and out of the circle.

Progression

- Create a dance based on the following:
  - the land is very dry, a raindrop falls
  - the raindrops come and go, fast and slow
  - muddy puddles trickle and grow
  - the puddles get bigger and bigger
  - puddles burst and streams flow
  - water, water everywhere!

'Stamping in puddles' using hoops.

Patterns and pathways

AIR AND FLOOR PATTERNS

FOLLOW-MY-LEADER PATHWAYS

PATTERNS AND PATHWAYS

CIRCLES AND SPIRALS

AN IMAGINARY JOURNEY

This section concentrates on the shape, size, direction, level and focus of movement. It introduces straight and curved patterns and pathways using varied stimulus ideas.

Air and floor patterns

Teaching points

- Introduce a variety of patterns by sitting down together and using one finger to draw patterns in the air. Begin with long, slow, straight lines contrasted by short, quick, zig-zagging lines.
- Once these air patterns are established, the children could interpret them with whole body actions. For example, stretching and shrinking on the spot or moving smoothly, then jerkily.
- Create a sequence of six stretching and shrinking actions. Vary the body shapes by asking for straight, smooth, jerky, sharp, curved, slow, wavy and fast actions. The children could practise on the spot alone, then with a partner. They could try to copy their partner's sequence.

Progression

- Add travelling to the sequence. The children could run in long, straight lines with crisp 'statue stops' and sudden changes of direction. They could jump in spiky, jagged shapes, turn on the spot and move in and out of other children.

Drawing patterns with fingers and then interpreting them with their bodies.

Follow-my-leader pathways

A ◆ I ◆ M

To use follow-my-leader games to create contrasting floor patterns.

RESOURCES

A white or black board
Percussion
Letter shapes

Teaching points

● Sit in a class group and draw patterns together in the air. The children could:
  – mirror the patterns that the teacher draws
  – draw letter and number shapes
  – write 'names' in the air.
  Encourage them to make large, exaggerated actions.

● Choose one of the patterns as the basis for a floor pattern. Try to vary the speed (for example, a slow, slithering 's' and a jumping jerky 'j') and the size (for example, an enormous 'o' and a little 'x').

● Play follow-my-leader games to show how contrasting air patterns can be traced as floor patterns. Head the line yourself until the pathway is established. Create links with 'how' to move and 'where' to go by:
  – running in long, straight lines with a sudden, sharp turn to face a new direction
  – hopping and jumping in short, zig-zagging lines
  – twisting and turning slowly in circles and spirals.

Progression

● Change leaders frequently. Stress simplicity and clarity so that the whole class can follow the action.

● Play follow-my-leader games in small groups. Activities could include:
  – skipping in circles and figures of eight
  – tiptoeing along straight 'tightrope' pathways
  – creeping along twisting lines, weaving in and out of spaces.

● Ask groups that show originality, clarity of action and pathway to give a demonstration.

Playing follow-my-leader games.

Circles and spirals

A ◆ I ◆ M

To use objects as the stimulus for turning and unravelling actions.

RESOURCES

Music (*Tubular Bells* by Mike Oldfield) or hand-held percussion

Teaching points

- Show examples of spirals (such as a spring, a shell, a screw or a spiral cut out of paper).
- Start in one large circle and lead the class slowly around and around the circle clockwise.
- Change direction (anti-clockwise) and lead the class in ever-decreasing circles towards the centre of the room.
- Repeat with each child holding on to the shoulder of the child in front. Elect one child as a leader. The spiralling pattern can be unwound by everyone turning on the spot to face the opposite way so that the end of the line leads.
- In small groups, give them the task of ravelling and unravelling the spiral.
- Space out and sit down. Use arm gestures to explore the changes in speed, size and strength that are possible when spiralling on the spot. Explore the spiralling gestures as whole body actions, such as: high wide, low curled, slow high and sudden low.

Progression

- Explore moving in lines, circles and spirals in small groups.
- Work alone, with a partner or with the whole class on the spot. Use contrasting travelling actions, speeds and strengths.

Forming spiral patterns on the spot.

An imaginary journey

A ◆ I ◆ M

To use props to reinforce the words 'over', 'under', 'around', 'through' and 'between'.

Teaching points

- Experiment with travelling in contrasting ways. For instance, along curved and straight pathways and at high levels. Stop the action frequently to check the spacing and level.
- Create an imaginary journey by playing a steady drumbeat and using the words 'over', 'around', 'towards', 'under', 'through' and 'away from'.
- Introduce apparatus to make this journey more interesting. Use music as a 'controlling' influence and ask for slow, careful actions as the children move through hoops, along benches, over each other, and under, around and between gymnastic apparatus.
- Create a repeatable sequence with changes in speed, level and direction.

Progression

- Use hoops, ropes, elastic, chalked pathways and parachute-type pieces of material to move in and out of, towards and away from, along, around, beneath and above.
- Develop this into a dance form using balances, jumps, falls, rolls, stretches, twists and bends.

RESOURCES

A tambourine
Drumbeat
Hoops
Benches
Simple gymnastic apparatus
Music (*Oxygène* by Jean-Michel Jarre)

Exploring action words such as 'under' and 'along'.

Magic and mystery

THE HAUNTED HOUSE

GHOSTLY CREATURES

MAGIC AND
MYSTERY

MAGIC MOMENTS

NIGHT-TIME SHADOWS

This section provides an imaginative framework within which the children are
encouraged to find many different ways to express changes in shape and size.

The haunted house

<table>
<tr><td>

A ◆ I ◆ M

To create 'surprises' within movement phrases.

</td><td>

RESOURCES

Music (*Oxygène* by Jean-Michel Jarre)
Drawing
Percussion

</td></tr>
</table>

Teaching points

- Indicate a focal point that represents the 'door' to the haunted house (for example, the centre of a class circle). The class could take a step and gesture towards it. Repeat these advancing and retreating actions several times saying 'push' and 'release'.
- Individually, creep to the space, then step forward and slowly, but strongly, push the door open using hands. Shoulders, legs and then backs could also be used. Create a surprise ending to this sequence by falling, rolling or staggering to represent the door opening.
- Explore the haunted house with creeping steps at high and low levels. Create frequent 'freezes' to check spacing and levels. Act out an imaginary meeting with ghostly creatures.
- Climb a spiral staircase by creating small follow-my-leader groups that creep around and around in small, spiralling circles.

Progression

- In small groups, set the task of finding a way out of the haunted house. Add percussion or stop the music so the children can create 'surprises'.
- Repeat with half the class stretched out to make a cobweb. The other half could creep carefully in and out of the 'web'.

Exploring a haunted house, 'freezing' when meeting ghosts.

Ghostly creatures

A ◆ I ◆ M	RESOURCES

A ◆ I ◆ M

To use voice sounds to accompany the action and to create 'surprises'.

RESOURCES

Music (*Tubular Bells* by Mike Oldfield)
Voice sounds such as 'oooh', 'eeeh', 'aaah'

Teaching points

- Pretend to be cobwebs, growing slowly from low, curled shapes into high, wide shapes. Stretch out to make a group web shape. (Repeat the giant cobweb activity from page 29.)
- A wispy, whirling ghost: shrink suddenly to the floor, then grow slowly with fingers and elbows leading into stretched, spiky or curved shapes.
- Spiders: stretch on to spidery hands and feet, then scuttle suddenly sideways while keeping that body shape. Develop to create giant spiders that creep quietly and scuttle suddenly.
- Skeletons: imagine bony arms, rattling kneebones and shaking skulls. Grow slowly or jump up on straight, stretched legs and loose, dangly shoulders with bent elbows and floppy fingers. Perform jerky, jolting skeleton dances alone and then in pairs.
- A big, black, magic cat: curl and stretch the 'paws' and then the whole body as well as running and stopping with 'paws' held high in the air. Make sudden statue stops and frequent changes in direction.
- Form a phrase of movement, such as, 'creep-creep-creep-pounce'.

Progression

- Divide the class into four groups of ghosts, spiders, skeletons and cats. Each group moves in turn. Then the children swirl into low shapes in an individual space ready to finish in a giant cobweb group shape.

Pretending to be big, black magic cats, curling and stretching.

FOLENS PE – *Dance* © Folens (copiable page)

Magic moments

A · I · M

To create opportunities for paired work through the 'witches and wizards' theme.

RESOURCES

A magic hat
A 'brew pot'

Teaching points

- Use the 'magic hat' to introduce the idea of moving in all sorts of ways as different creatures and characters. The children could pretend to be frogs jumping, spiders scuttling, bats balancing, skeletons jerking and jolting, ghosts swirling and cats creeping. Change activities frequently and improve the quality, showing clear examples.
- Witches: move spiky body parts in isolation to make crooked, irregular shapes. Stop silently and then freeze and 'scoop' at high and low levels as though secretly gathering ingredients for a magic brew.
- Wizards: rise slowly from low, curled shapes to high stretched shapes with an imaginary cloak held firmly in the fingers. Turn on the spot quickly and slowly and move into spaces. Introduce 'shifty' eyes that move from side to side.
- Contrast the spiky jerky movement of the witch and the strong bold strides and short shuffling 'wizard steps'. The children's imaginary cloaks should be in action. Divide the class into witches and wizards, with each group moving in turn.

Gathering imaginary
ingredients for
a magic 'brew pot'.

Progression

- Develop a sequence in pairs. The children could step silently as though looking for ingredients to put in a 'magic brew', then freeze and secretly snatch an imaginary object into their cloak.
- Finish with the 'brew pot' in the centre of the circle and the children dancing as witches and wizards around it.

Night-time shadows

To recall and repeat aspects of this section spontaneously in pairs.

RESOURCES

Voice sounds
Percussion

Making a shadow dance.

Teaching points

- The children could perform mirror images by copying your hand gestures and then growing and shrinking into mirror images of your shapes, such as high, low or twisted.
- Repeat this work in pairs. The children mirror each other and then play follow-my-leader shadows. The 'leader' steps slowly, then stretches, curls or twists into a shape that the 'follower' copies.
- Play a simple game of trying to escape from shadows.
- Explore the action ideas in the shadowy rhyme below.

Progression

- Use mirroring and shadowing ideas to explore some 'ghostly creatures':
  - wispy, whirly ghosts: shrink suddenly to the floor, then grow closely with fingertips leading into wide shapes. Then, curling and swirling at high and low levels, move slowly and suddenly from space to space with opening and closing arms.
  - skeletons: grow into skeleton shapes and collapse again.
- Using loose, dangly shoulders, bent elbows and floppy fingers, create a jolting, jerky skeleton dance with bent body parts.
- Create a dance that alternates between shadowy ghosts and spooky skeletons. Create other imaginary ghostly creatures. Make voice sounds to accompany the action.

Shadow

*Shadow, shadow curled up small,
I can make you grow up tall.*

*Now we're jumping
stretched out wide,
Shadow, shadow at my side.*

*Tiptoe slowly, shadow go,
I can't lose my shadow though.*

Animals

CATS

THE ZOO

ANIMALS

CARNIVAL OF THE ANIMALS 1

CARNIVAL OF THE ANIMALS 2

This section focuses on animals. It culminates in a 'carnival of the animals' accompanied by the music of Saint-Saëns.

Cats

RESOURCES

Word and voice sounds
Music (from *Cats* by Andrew
Lloyd Webber)
Hoop

Teaching points

● Stretch and curl into cat shapes. Curl,
arch or stretch from low shapes on the
floor to wide, outstretched shapes on
hands and feet or high on tiptoes.
● Isolate the paws and claws by suddenly
popping each finger out of the fist in
turn. Repeat this with legs and toes.
● Form phrases of creeping and freezing,
creeping and leaping, leaping
and pouncing.
● Use this rhythm to form a short
dance in pairs, about cats:

> *Quietly creeping,*
> *Curling, rolling,*
> *Leap and twirl away.*

● Develop an action-reaction dance
between two cats. Move one at a time.
Create changes in speed, level
and direction.

Progression

● Improvise in pairs, using appropriate
voice sounds to represent cats
meeting one another. Contrast
creeping slowly with running fast,
sudden pouncing with stillness,
fast turning with slow sinking.
● Divide into small groups and give
each group a hoop to represent a
dustbin. Ask the 'cats' to move in
and out, creep around and appear
above and below the hoop 'dustbin'.

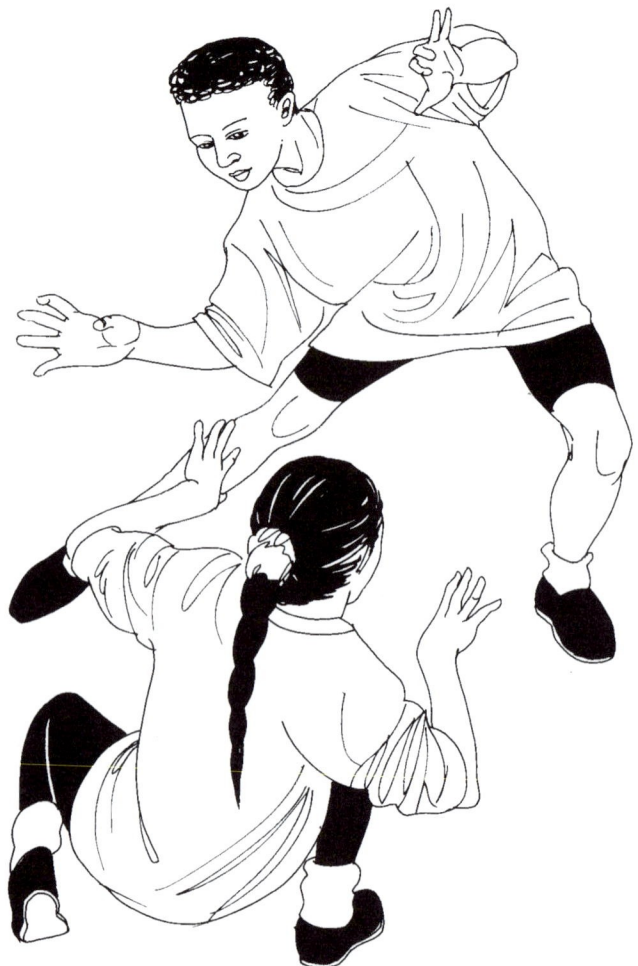

Reacting to each other as cats.

The zoo

RESOURCES

Percussion
Voice sounds

Teaching points

- Start with varied travelling activities, including running, creeping, leaping, hopping, galloping and trotting. Create clear stopping points to check the spacing.
- Introduce animal categories for the children to explore, such as:
  - creeping, crawling creatures
  - prowling, growling creatures
  - tiny, scuttling creatures
  - enormous, clumsy creatures
  - slippery, sliding creatures
  - fluttering, flying creatures.
- Divide the class into six groups. Each group could concentrate on one of the above categories. Ask for simple travelling phrases in follow-my-leader formations.

Progression

- Create a class composition. Each group performs its phrase, then, with the teacher as leader, the groups join together to form one long follow-my-leader line.
- Each animal category could lead the line while the rest of the class follow. The class line could creep and crawl, then prowl and growl, scuttle and stop, plod and stamp, slither and slide and finally flutter and fly.
- Finish with a free choice of animal category.

Exploring movements in animal categories.

Carnival of the animals 1

A ◆ I ◆ M

To create animal shapes and actions alone, then in small groups.

RESOURCES

Music (*Carnival of the Animals* by Saint-Saëns)

Teaching points

● Recall the animal action categories from page 35 and practise these individually.

● Play Saint-Saëns' *Carnival of the Animals* to explore different animals.

● *The royal march of the lion*: march around the room with heads held high, toes pointed and arms clawing the air. When the music roars, rise up with faces to the ceiling to 'roar'. Finish with long, light runs from paw to paw.

● *The aviary*: make stretching and swooping actions from low curled to high wide to low shapes. Include a running phrase on the 'swoop', flying and fluttering with arms rising and stretching, sinking and closing. Create running phrases with balanced 'fluttering' freezes.

● *Graceful giraffes*: balance on tiptoes with long stretched necks, arms and legs and then move with graceful trotting actions to the music.

Progression

● Create crocodile lines of groups of three. The first child should use 'open' and 'closed' arms to make 'jaws', the middle child should use outstretched arms and fingers as 'claws' and the last child should pretend to move with big, bent back 'legs'. Each crocodile group should move slowly as one unit, changing leaders so that each child has the chance to be all parts.

Marching as lions, clawing the air and roaring.

Carnival of the animals 2

A · I · M

To initiate, recreate and invent animal actions.

RESOURCES

Music (*Carnival of the Animals* by Saint-Saëns)

Teaching points

- Start with the class in a circle. Form a class follow-my-leader line and imitate 'animal' actions, such as quiet creeping, strong stamping, powerful prowling, sudden scuttling, rhythmic trotting and graceful galloping.
- Change leaders every time the activity changes.
- Pretend to be enormous elephants. Plod individually with wide, flat feet, broad, bent backs and with one arm extended to form a long trunk.
- Create 'elephants' in pairs. Plod towards a partner, then stand one behind the other, holding one arm out in front for a trunk, the other arm behind for a tail. Join trunks and tails by holding hands and then plod, jog or dance together in elephant lines.
- Pretend to be kangaroos. Jump from two feet to two feet in and out of spaces. Contrast big, bouncy jumps with little, light jumps, all with fists, elbows and knees bent.

Imitating animal actions.

Progression

- Select one child to march like a lion. When the leader marches by, each child joins to form one long, class line.
- Change leaders frequently, introducing a new animal activity for each leader.
- Introduce some 'new' animals, such as:
  - monkeys as amazing acrobats that can balance, cartwheel, jump, fall and roll
  - penguins waddling in small, squat shapes with turned-out, flat, flopping feet and puffed-out tummies.

  Make a group circle and jump in and out of a 'pond' to finish the lesson.

Minibeasts

MINIBEASTS

THE BIRTH OF THE BUTTERFLY

MINIBEASTS

POND LIFE

THE SPIDER AND THE FLY

In this section the movement characteristics of different types of insect are explored. The emphasis is on creating dances in class groups.

Minibeasts

<table>
<tr><td>

A ◆ I ◆ M

To introduce minibeasts through running, creeping, jumping, slithering and flying activities.

</td><td>

RESOURCES

Percussion sounds
Music (*Soil festivities* by Vangelis)

</td></tr>
</table>

Teaching points

- Introduce minibeasts using running, creeping, jumping, slithering and flying activities. Create pauses to check the spacing and use examples to improve the quality of movements.
- Organise the class into small groups so the children can explore in more detail.
- Ants: include scurrying walkers and 'soldier' ants marching up and down, protecting an imaginary queen.
- Worms: practise slithering, sliding and burrowing in and out of the soil.
- Spiders: creep forwards and backwards, spinning webs from high to low on the spot and then forming a group web.
- Centipedes: divide the children into groups to create a follow-my-leader line.
- Fleas: jump towards and away from each other.

Making slithering, burrowing movements like worms in the soil.

Progression

- Use music to create a minibeast 'parade' with the children in group lines. Each group moves in turn, creeping, jumping, flying, running and slithering.
- Make one enormous 'ant hill'. One child stands in the centre of the room while the others make curled shapes around the edge. Touch every other child in the circle. They should creep towards the child in the middle. Ensure that the children are a good distance apart.
- Form the 'ant hill' by growing slowly upwards in unison. Move with backs leading and heads tucked in. Repeat, with those in the centre rising higher than the rest.

The birth of a butterfly

<table>
<tr><td>A ◆ I ◆ M

To create a 'class' movement piece with opportunities for individual and group interpretation.</td></tr>
</table>

Teaching points

- Start with a sequence of floor-based actions that represent the movements of a caterpillar. Stretch slowly from curled shapes, arching, shrinking and curling again.
- In groups of three, improvise around the idea of 'weaving a cocoon'. Turn slowly and spiral from low to high levels. Form a trio line and explore spiralling together inwards, then outwards, until a spiral-shaped cocoon is formed.
- Explore the 'birth' of a butterfly individually and then reform into trios to create a bigger butterfly with one child as the body and the other two as the wings. Work in stages.
- Wings unfolding: use strong, pushing actions and move from curled shapes with elbows and arms slowly unfurling.
- Wings fluttering: balance on the spot with sudden, fluttering actions of the arms (wings) and intermittent stops.
- Butterflies: run and stretch upwards, then glide to a low level with arms closing around the body. Use the words 'fly', 'float' and 'settle' to improve the quality of the action.

RESOURCES

Photographs of a caterpillar cocoon and butterfly

Using slow curling stretches to represent a butterfly.

Progression

- Create a class dance based on the 'birth of a butterfly'. Start with individual butterflies stretching, running, fluttering and curling from space to space.
- In small groups, allow the children freedom of interpretation. Work towards forming a repeatable sequence of movements that can be performed to the class. Use pauses to attract attention to important shapes, for example, caterpillar, cocoon and butterfly.

Pond life

A ◆ I ◆ M

To develop small group dances that will be combined to form a class group dance.

RESOURCES

Action poem (below)

Teaching points

- Start in a space in a low, curled shape. Move lightly up and down into a new space with sudden, spiky actions. Jump with knees bent and elbows jutting out, suddenly gesturing with one arm and then leaping to a new space to create an element of surprise.
- In groups of three, create opening and closing shapes. Then rotate a wide open group shape into another space and repeat the sequence.
- Create groups of six by joining the trios and working on circular floor patterns, circles, criss-cross shapes and high and low spirals. Stop in an underwater web shape.
- Explore moving across the floor with smooth, creeping steps. Move face down, then on backs with arms and legs splayed.
- Contrast the smooth gliding steps on their fronts with the fast, frantic steps on their backs.

Progression

- Each group chooses one action, such as spiders or beetles. Each one moves in turn.
- Form a dance in six parts. Use the above ideas to create individual and group compositions based on the poem *Life in the pond!*

Jumping with knees bent and gesturing with arms.

Life in the pond!

The water of the pond is still.
There is no sign of life.
Except for a ripple, a raindrop,
a fish darting, a frog jumping.
There are floating water lilies.
The flowers turn their heads to the sun.
The water spider spins a web among
the water plants.
The water beetle swings under water
on its front and on its back.
It flies about the pond.
The spring pond is alive!

The spider and the fly

A ◆ I ◆ M

To explore the differences between shape- and action-based activity using the web (shape) and the fly (action).

RESOURCES

A cymbal

Teaching points

● Introduce the action of spiders. Explore different balances, using one, two, three or four limbs. Balance and then curl and stretch into the next shape. Find new transitions between balancing shapes and contrasts in fast and slow actions.

● Form a 'super spider' sequence by:
- stretching out on hands and feet or on two wide feet only with back bent and arms reaching
- stepping slowly with exaggerated steps and wide, stretched feet and fingers
- curling, rolling and then stretching to start the sequence again.

● Introduce 'Flit, the fearless fly', who rises on tiptoes with bent, elbow wings and spiky fingers. Run from place to place, 'flitting' quickly and quietly.

● In groups of three, weave a spider's web by curling up close together, then stretching and growing into wide, stretched 'balancing' shapes. Older children could try 'counter-balances' with each other.

● Use elastic to experiment with stretched-out shapes that reach high and low and form criss-cross patterns.

● Stretch together in unison, then one at a time so that a web shape is formed.

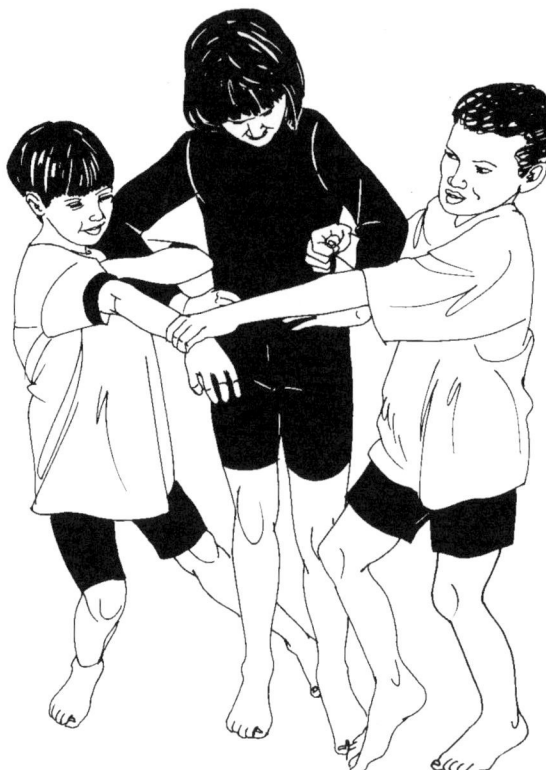

Weaving webs in groups of three.

Progression

● Choose several groups to be wide, web shapes (with or without elastic). The rest are individual flies. The flies run from space to space and the webs slowly change level and shape. The flies run in and out of the webs and stop and start frequently.

● Make a class cobweb that grows at the same time. Then try 'growing' one strand at a time by tiptoeing and touching the children one by one. When touched, the children stretch slowly into web shapes.

Carnival time

CLOWNS

A FANCY DRESS PARADE

CARNIVAL TIME!

A CARNIVAL FAIRGROUND

THE CARNIVAL PARADE

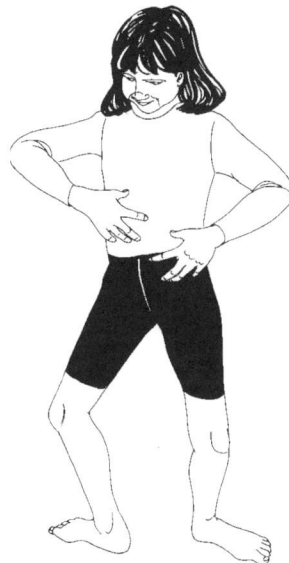

This section is the culmination of the book. It provides an imaginative framework within which the children are encouraged to find many different ways to express changes in shape, size, strength and rhythm, working alone and with others.

Clowns

A ◆ I ◆ M

To improvise around the
theme to form simple
clowning sequences.

RESOURCES

Music (silent movie
piano-style pieces)
A cymbal or drum

Teaching points

- Play the music to introduce a dancing carnival parade, including skipping, dancing, jumping and clapping in and out of spaces. Change leader and activities frequently.
- Call in the clowns. Make wide body shapes with puffed tummies and cheeks and flat, wide feet. Work on 'funny walks' with lifted knees and exaggerated actions.
- Talk about different types of clowns. Encourage a variety, such as silly, sensible, sad, or acrobatic.
- For acrobatic clowns, explore balancing in standing, kneeling and floor-bound shapes. Create transitions between balances using jumping, falling, turning and rolling actions.
- Use three balances and two transitions to create a sequence of acrobatic clown movements. The action should contain pauses and changes in speed, including 'slow motion'. Use exaggerated body shapes, with angular knees, elbows, wrists and ankles.

Using exaggerated walks to imitate clowns.

Progression

- Improvise simple dance sequences that involve all the 'clowning' elements explored in the lesson.
- Create a custard pie routine! In pairs, the children could be clowns showing off one by one. Then perform a 'stretch-throw-shrink' custard pie fight. Finally clean up by pulling the mess from faces and fingers. Repeat the whole routine in slow motion.

A fancy-dress parade

A ◆ I ◆ M	RESOURCES
To gain an understanding of pausing after each series of movements.	Percussion Music (steel band and Latin American music) Fancy-dress costumes

Teaching points

- Play follow-my-leader. Start by tiptoeing around the class touching each child on the shoulder. When touched, each child follows. Change leaders and activities frequently. The children could march, stride, hop, or jump.
- In pairs, recreate the clown sequence from page 44 as a slow-motion repeat.
- The children could become fancy-dress characters such as witches, wizards, magicians or film and cartoon characters. In small groups, form a short parade sequence. For example, crooked witches stirring the magic brew and then dancing around the cauldron, or crazy cartoon characters with animal masks and exaggerated creeping, leaping, pouncing and pausing actions.
- Develop a pantomime horse. In pairs, the child in front nods his or her head and the partner swings his or her hips to imitate the swish of the horse's tail. Move together as a unit. A large piece of material draped over them will help to make a horse.

The children become fancy-dress characters.

Progression

- Develop the pantomime horse dance ensuring that each child has a turn at leading. Encourage the use of different pathways.

- Finish the lesson with a fancy-dress parade to the music. Use statue stops to check that the children are remaining 'in character'.

A carnival fairground

A ◆ I ◆ M
To create circle dances in large and small groups.

RESOURCES

Photo or diagram of
group circle
Hoops

Teaching points

● Sit and clap various rhythmic patterns in one big class circle. Stand and stamp out these patterns. Finally, form short rhythmic phrases, such as 'stamp-stamp-stamp-clap', in and out of the class circle shape. Repeat several times to give the feeling of moving as one big group in unison.

● Spread out into a big circle and stand facing the middle. Make a roundabout by forming a follow-my-leader circle, all facing the same way. Then trot, tiptoe, march and skip clockwise, then anti-clockwise, around the circle.

● In smaller groups, explore different types of roundabout circles. For example, imitate horses rising, sinking and trotting or an aeroplane rising, sinking and swooping, and so on.

● Form group lines. Place hoops on the floor as roundabouts. Accompany the action with percussion. Each group could tiptoe, march, trot, skip or gallop from hoop to hoop, circling each one in turn. Create clear pauses and emphasise moving from hoop to hoop as though moving from ride to ride.

Hoops can be used in various ways in circle dances.

Progression

● Lead the class into a big roundabout circle again and stretch out wide to form a Big Wheel. Try rotating slowly sideways in this shape.

● Select children to create a smaller circle inside the big wheel and give them hoops. Explore rotating in different ways and changing levels to represent roundabout mechanisms.

The carnival parade

<table>
<tr><td>

A ◆ I ◆ M

To create imaginary fancy dress characters and to move appropriately – alone then with others.

</td></tr>
</table>

Steel band sounds or Latin American folk music, such as The Gypsy Kings
A cymbal or drum

Teaching points

- Play follow-my-leader with different children leading the line. Each child chooses different travelling activities and starting and stopping shapes.
- In groups of three or five, imagine fancy-dress people, such as witches and wizards, cartoon or fairy-tale characters. Parade and show the sequence to the others.
- Be acrobats and clowns. Allow individual choice and choose examples of quality to improve the standard and scope of the rest. Refer to previous sessions on funny ways of walking, balancing and acrobatic actions.
- Become limbo dancers. Two children hold a bamboo cane. The rest of the class take it in turns to practise the real limbo! In pairs, perform an exaggerated version of the limbo. Finally form groups of four with one pair clapping and dancing while the other pair limbo. Change around at frequent intervals.

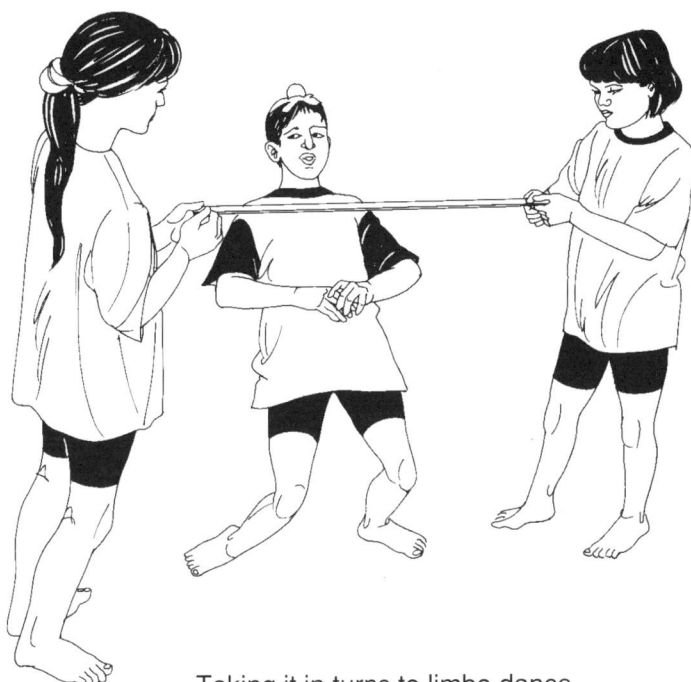

Taking it in turns to limbo dance.

Progression

- Introduce 'animal masks' and refer back to pages 36–37.
- Choose two children to be important lions marching with paws clawing through the air and pausing to roar.

- Other children could be mischievous monkeys who jump and bounce with long arms swinging from side to side. Develop paired work using travelling activities, such as running, galloping and jumping.
- Finish with a 'mighty monster' or a 'class caterpillar'. Step slowly in a follow-my-leader line, pause, sway, sink, rise and roar in unison.

Dance evaluation sheet

● In your lesson today did you:

- warm up with one of the following:

  travel?   turn?

  jump?   gesture?

- understand the dance idea and find movements to express this?

- put forward original and creative ideas?

- work alone, with a partner or in a small or large group?

- remember your sequence or dance and repeat it several times?

- memorise a movement or step pattern?

- perform your dance in front of others?

- watch others and make fair comments about their performance?

- learn something new?

- perform your dance work the way you wanted to? If not, how?

● Describe the lesson in words or with a drawing.